39

Chicago Postwar Passenger and Commuter Trains

John Kelly

Iconografix

Iconografix
1830A Hanley Road
Hudson, Wisconsin 54016 USA

Library of Congress Control Number: 2012931302

ISBN-10: 1-58388-291-X
ISBN-13: 978-1-58388-291-7

12 13 14 15 16 17 6 5 4 3 2 1

Printed in The United States of America

Layout by St. Croix Art & Design, Osceola, WI.
www.stcroixart.com

Cover photo: The Rock Island Railroad and Southern Pacific Lines operated the Golden State passenger train between Chicago and Los Angeles. On a cold, clear Chicago winter day the Golden State departed LaSalle Station led by Rock Island E8 in maroon-and-yellow wings scheme, circa 1960s. *J. M. Gruber collection*

Table of Contents:

Acknowledgements

My first book on *Chicago Stations and Trains* focused on the history and architecture of Chicago's six railroad stations. The book was well-received and after talking with my publisher (Iconografix), I decided to write this book on *Chicago Postwar Passenger and Commuter Trains.*

Chicago is my favorite big city to visit and I always travel there by train. In the past, I commuted via Chicago & North Western's Northwest Line from Harvard, Illinois, to North Western Station in downtown Chicago. Recently I began riding Amtrak's Hiawatha Service from downtown Milwaukee to Chicago Union Station. When Amtrak Hiawatha-Train 334 arrived on Track 17 at Union Station's North Concourse, Metra diesel locomotives were idling with their commuter trains on adjacent tracks. I enjoyed walking with the other passengers into the grand, Beaux-Arts style station. Built during the Roaring Twenties and the Jazz Age, opened July 23, 1925, Union Station's colonnaded-fronted head-house takes you back to the era when passenger trains provided an efficient and economical means of transportation in the United States. Today, Chicago Union Station serves as Amtrak's Midwest hub for intercity and regional trains plus Metra commuter trains.

Thanks to my good friend J.M. Gruber (Mainline Photos) for sharing his wonderful Chicago passenger train photos. John Mummert contributed Amtrak "Rainbow Era" pictures, and Joe Piersen (Chicago & North Western Historical Society) provided C&NW commuter train images.

Philip Weibler assisted with historical information, and Dennis McClendon of Chicago CartoGraphics provided the circa 1945 stations map. Special thanks to Arthur Miller, Archivist and Librarian for Special Collections at Lake Forest College, and John Gruber (Center for Railroad Photography & Art) in Madison, Wisconsin, for their support. As always, to my partner and train riding companion Linda Shult for her proofreading skills and to Iconografix for publishing this book.

John Kelly
Madison, Wisconsin

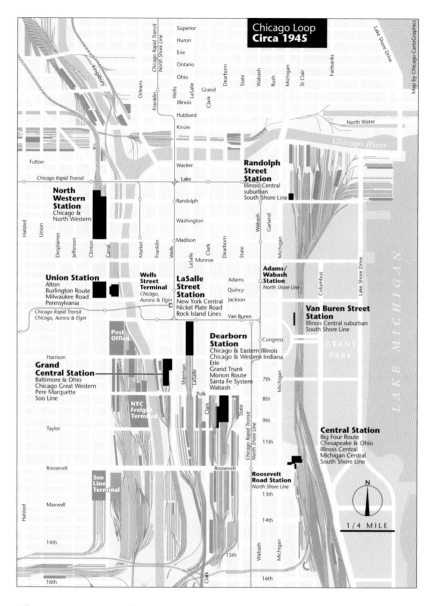

Chicago Loop and Stations map, circa 1945. *Courtesy Dennis McClendon, Chicago CartoGraphics*

Introduction

Post-World War II Chicago experienced prosperity, peaceful times and a population boom from 3,300,000 million in 1940 to 3,620,000 by 1950. The city enjoyed a surge of economic and industrial growth when servicemen returned in 1945. Patriotism was high and big changes were happening all across the city in the way its citizens lived, worked and traveled. War rationing had created pent-up demand for steel, rubber and other supplies. Even before the war had ended, the War Production Board reduced the capacity for raw materials and war manufactured goods by 35 percent, allowing thousands of new railroad passenger cars to be built. Orders for the new passenger cars brought much needed work to Pullman-Standard on Chicago's south side. Most major railroads serving Chicago, including New York Central and Santa Fe, upgraded their passenger fleets with lightweight, streamlined cars. Wabash Railroad considered a new seven-car streamliner and Rock Island Railroad requested bids for cars to enlarge its Rocket fleet. Several Chicago area railroads including Chicago & North Western planned to enlarge their coach and service facilities, anticipating upgrades to their passenger fleets.

Optimism was high among railroads as orders for new locomotives went to General Motors Electro-Motive Division, American Locomotive and Baldwin Locomotive Works. As the railroads anxiously awaited their modern locomotives and streamlined passenger cars to arrive, *Trains* magazine (August 1948) cover story was *Chicago: Railroad Capital of the World.* The article stated, "Chicago…gathering place of the railroads…22 trunk lines, seven belt and switching roads, eight industrial railroads and three electric lines…Track everywhere, passenger trains and commuter trains crowding the approaches to the terminals near the Loop…as many as 10 passenger trains a minute arriving during the morning peak,

and 12 a minute leaving during the evening rush…that is Chicago, undisputed railroad capital of the world."

Arguable the best and busiest of Chicago's big six stations was Union Station, standing majestically on the Chicago River near the edge of the Loop district between Adams and Jackson Street. Union Station comprised two buildings: the head house and concourse. The colonnade-fronted head house on the west side of Canal Street provided eight stories for offices and featured a main waiting room (Great Hall) with 112-foot, vaulted ceiling and skylight plus ticket windows and Fred Harvey Lunch Room. The concourse building on the east side of Canal Street included baggage counters, information desk, newsstand, shops and train gates. An underground passageway connected both buildings with below-street-level track layouts in the form of two back-to-back, stub-end terminals, one facing north (nine tracks) and the other south (13 tracks). Two tracks adjacent to the Chicago River allowed run-through train operations when needed. Union Station was the Chicago terminal of four great railroads: the Pennsylvania; the Chicago, Burlington & Quincy; the Chicago, Milwaukee, St. Paul & Pacific; and Gulf, Mobile & Ohio. The station's slogan was "Cross-Roads of the Nation" and well-known passenger trains calling at the station included the Broadway Limited, California Zephyr, Empire Builder, North Coast Limited and Twin Cities Hiawatha.

Chicago's other five passenger train stations were the gates to everywhere with many "name" trains arriving and departing daily. Dearborn Station was the Chicago Terminal of the Santa Fe Railway and its flagship transcontinental Super Chief, often referred to as "Train of the Stars" for the movie-stars and celebrities who believed there was only one way, the Super Chief Way, to travel from Los Angeles to Chicago. Built in 1885 and located at South Dearborn and West Polk Street, it was originally known as Polk Street Station. Although it was the smallest of Chicago's big-six stations, Dearborn was the most cosmopolitan, boasting six carriers including Santa Fe, Chicago & Eastern Illinois, Erie, Grand Trunk, Monon, and Wabash. Today, Dearborn's head house still stands in the Printer's Row neighborhood among antique stores, book stores and condominiums. But, as part of Chicago's urban renewal, the train shed was torn down in 1976.

Grand Central Station was originally built for the Wisconsin Central Railroad and the Chicago and Northern Pacific Railroad in 1890. Following Wisconsin Central's financial troubles in 1910, control of the station passed to the Baltimore & Ohio Chicago Terminal Railroad.

Grand Central was located in the southwest part of the Chicago Loop between Harrison and Wells Street, along the south branch of the Chicago River. The station was designed in a traditional L-shape with the waiting room facing Wells Street and a carriage court along Harrison Street. The magnificent, barrel-vaulted steel and glass train shed spanned six tracks and at the time of its construction was the second largest built (after Grand Central in New York). The station's outstanding feature was the 247-foot tower clock with B&O herald greeting passengers. Visitors remarked that Grand Central Station reminded them of a cathedral with beautiful stained-glass windows and ornate, iron gates leading to the trains. Baltimore & Ohio's Capitol Limited was the premier train calling at Grand Central. Other roads included Chicago Great Western, Pere Marquette and Soo Line. It was the least busy of Chicago's six stations. Following Grand Central's closing on November 8, 1969, B&O and C&O trains transferred to Chicago & North Western Station until they were discontinued with the beginning of Amtrak in 1971. Described by the *Chicago Tribune* as "decaying, dreary and sadly out of date," Grand Central Station was razed in 1971.

Central Station dates to 1893 and was the northern terminus for Illinois Central's "Main Line of Mid-America" passenger trains, located at the southern end of Grant Park at Roosevelt Road (12th Street) and Michigan Avenue. The nine-story station housed the general offices of the Illinois Central Railroad and featured a 13-story clock tower. For thousands of African Americans migrating north from the southern states of Louisiana and Mississippi, the clock tower and Illinois Central neon sign welcomed them to Chicago. And Central Station certainly provided the most scenic route into the Loop with views of Lake Michigan. Illinois Central's Panama Limited and fabled City of New Orleans used Central Station, as did New York Central subsidiary Michigan Central and Big Four Route. Central Station survived into the Amtrak era when the last trains departed March 6, 1972. The station was demolished in 1974 and today is the site of urban condominiums.

La Salle Station was built in 1903, and located in the center of Chicago's financial district at La Salle and Van Buren Street with the elevated transit system at its front door. The 12-story stone and brick station was headquarters for Rock Island Railroad's Rocket passenger trains and Golden State Limited. La Salle Station was also Chicago Division offices for Nickel Plate Road trains and New York Central's Great Steel Fleet, including the legendary 20th Century Limited. The station included two levels. Passenger ticket counters, baggage and mail facilities were on the first floor. On the second floor, reached by escalator, were the waiting room, concourse and tracks. In 1981, La Salle Station was torn down for the Chicago Stock Exchange and in its place a new commuter facility was built for Metra's Rock Island District trains.

When North Western Station (C&NW) on Madison and Canal Street opened in 1911, it was the largest of Chicago's passenger stations. Six approach tracks led to the station's 16 stub-end tracks under the 894-foot train shed. In addition to serving C&NW's extensive commuter fleet extending north, northwest and west from downtown Chicago, the station was also home terminal to the "400 Fleet" of Midwestern streamliners. From the 1930s until October 1955, C&NW participated in joint train operations from Chicago to Omaha with western railroads Union Pacific and Southern Pacific. Famous name trains arriving and departing from North Western Station were the City of Los Angeles, City of San Francisco, City of Portland, City of Denver and Challenger. In 1984, the station's head house was demolished and a modern glass-sheathed office tower was built. In 1997 it was named the Ogilvie Transportation Center, and today hosts Metra commuter trains operating on Union Pacific lines (former C&NW).

While Chicago's big six stations continued to operate into the 60s, the decline of American passenger trains really began much er. In his book, *Twilight of the Great Trains* (Kalmbach Books) r Fred Frailey states, "In 1944 near the end of World War II, ercent of intercity rail travel by public transport was by rail. 1949 the rail share had fallen to 48 percent, and by 1960 to 29 ercent." Several factors contributed to this down turn. Americans' mode of travel changed as soldiers returned from war, got married, started families and moved to the newly developed suburbs. After passage of the Federal-Aid Highway Act in 1956, the Interstate Highway System was built. Detroit automakers were busy selling family station wagons and other gas-guzzlers with the promise of cheap gasoline forever. And the fast-paced growth of the airline industry offered lower fares and faster flying times to the same cities served by passenger trains. By 1960, American passenger train service was dismal as people drove new cars or took commercial air travel to their destinations. The railroads responded by petitioning the Interstate Commerce Commission to discontinue many marginal trains serving smaller cities. Although many of the "name" trains (that were re-equipped after the war with new locomotives and cars) remained in service, they were showing their age. The final blow came in October of 1967, when the U.S. Postal Service cancelled its first-class mail haulage contracts with the railroads in favor of trucks and airplanes. Second and third-class mail continued to be carried by rail but that was not enough to save the passenger trains.

So "All Aboard" from Chicago, Illinois, as we ride those colorful streamliners named Broadway Limited, 20th Century Limited, Capitol Limited, California Zephyr, Denver Zephyr, Empire Builder, Golden State, Hiawatha, North Coast Limited, Panama Limited, Rocket, South Wind, San Francisco Chief, 400, and Union Pacific "City" trains into their twilight years.

Chicago Union Station – Cross-Roads of the Nation

"Cross-Roads of the Nation" picture booklet was published by the Chicago Union Station Company, April 1955. It described the large passenger terminal and the four great railroads that used its services. *Author collection*

WAY OF THE

Burlington Route

Zephyrs

AMERICA'S DISTINCTIVE TRAINS

Chicago Union Station opened July 23, 1925, and is located along Canal Street on the west side of the Chicago River's south branch. The Renaissance-style, colonnade-fronted structure was designed as two buildings by Chicago architect Daniel Burnham. The head house building faced Canal Street and the Concourse building fronted the Chicago River. *Zephyr ticket folder, Author collection*

CHICAGO UNION STATION

From this huge passenger terminal, trains of four great railroads span the nation

THE CONCOURSE

Standing majestically on the Chicago river at the edge of the famous "Loop" district is the $90 million structure of stone, steel and concrete that is Chicago's finest and most modern railroad passenger terminal—The Chicago Union Station.

From this convenient location at the edge of the busy downtown area, passengers may board streamlined, diesel-powered passenger trains of four great railroads—the Pennsylvania, the Chicago, Burlington & Quincy, the Chicago, Milwaukee, St. Paul & Pacific and the Gulf, Mobile & Ohio—and travel, literally, to the ends of America; to the Atlantic or the Pacific, to Canada or Mexico. Yet Chicago Union Station is almost a city in itself for within its 35 acres of property, more than 1,500 people earn their livelihood serving railroad travelers.

The present station buildings are erected on the site of two previous Union Stations. The first structure, built in 1858, and the second, in 1880 by the Pittsburgh, Fort Wayne and Chicago Railroad (now part of the Pennsylvania). The great Chicago fire destroyed the original station in 1871. The second, completed in

1880, was, in its day, considered a splendid terminal. It was used also by the Burlington, the Milwaukee and the then Chicago & Alton (now G.M.& O.) on a rental basis.

But the city of Chicago grew so rapidly that by 1912 it became apparent that a new, and greatly enlarged Union Station would be needed to serve its travel needs. In July, 1913, while many plans were being drawn up and considered, the present Chicago Union Station Company was formed to construct, maintain and operate the proposed new terminal. This company, owned together by the Pennsylvania, the Burlington and the Milwaukee, has successfully carried out this most complex assignment.

Train service was maintained without interruption during the intricate construction of the present buildings which began in 1914. Work, halted during World War I, was largely completed by 1925 and on May 17 of that year a man going to Pittsburgh, Pa., bought the first ticket sold in the new building. Since that time countless persons have come to the large ticket office to purchase safe, comfortable train travel to towns both far and near.

The following illustrations from "Cross-Roads of the Nation" booklet describe Chicago Union Station's huge passenger terminal and trains of four great railroads that span the nation. *Milwaukee Road ticket folder, Author collection*

THE LUNCH ROOM

Fred Harvey

The restaurants and shops in Chicago Union Station have been operated by Fred Harvey since the station opened in 1925. A wide choice of restaurants await the traveler. They include the club-like dining room, the popular lunch room and the large cafeteria—all serving full meals; and the Semaphore luncheonette, the Shoppers Mart soda fountain and the Iron Horse cocktail lounge. There are also private dining rooms for special parties and business meetings. And far out of sight in the basement driveway is a little snack counter for the convenience of taxicab and truck drivers. On a typical day these many Fred Harvey eating places in Chicago Union Station will serve more than 8,600 patrons!

Fred Harvey also operates the Shoppers Mart—offering a wide selection of domestic and imported gifts; three newsstands—where popular books, as well as newspapers and magazines are available; eight different cigar and cigarette stands, and a large, modern barber shop.

Behind the scenes, and beneath the main floor, are blocks of neat, orderly stockrooms, large gleaming kitchens, a bakery—and even a dairy! Dishes from the numerous restaurants travel to a centralized washing room on an elaborate automatic conveyor system.

THE SHOPPERS MART

The Fred Harvey System operated restaurants and newsstands in stations mostly along the Santa Fe Railway from Chicago to California. *Santa Fe train porter claim check, Author collection*

THE TICKET OFFICE

As many as 5,000 persons in a single day, may visit these windows of Union Station's large ticket office. And the ticket sellers behind the windows must know how to figure the correct fare to any city or village in The United States, Canada and Mexico—and do it quickly! For some passengers, they also reserve parlor car, or coach seats—or perhaps one of the nine different types of sleeping car accommodations that are offered by the Union Station railroads. In view of this, it is not surprising that there is sometimes a short wait for ticket service during a rush period.

THE BAGGAGE CHECK COUNTER

Railroads do not expect passengers to carry all of their suitcases and trunks with them on the train. Instead they have a baggage checking system which enables passengers to have a liberal quantity of luggage handled for them in baggage cars. Here, behind the windows of the checking counter, experienced baggage men carefully make out the cardboard checks that will guide each piece of luggage to its destination. Enroute, both in baggage cars and at stations where there might be a change of trains, records of each piece handled are carefully kept.

THE JAIL

While it seems unusual to have a jail in a railroad station, this two-cell lockup serves one very useful purpose. It is used as a "waiting room" for prisoners of the law who are being transported by train under police escort. It is one of the protective facilities maintained by the Chicago Union Station Company's police department, which also supervises auto traffic in the station driveways and maintains a constant patrol of all public rooms on the main floor. The department works closely with city, county, state and federal law enforcement agencies as well as the special agent and police departments of the railroads.

This illustration showed Chicago Union Stations ticket office, baggage claim counter and jail. *Burlington Route baggage tag, Author collection*

BEHIND THE SCENES

TRAIN STARTING SIGNAL

Unseen by passengers, yet vital to the everyday job at Chicago Union Station, are the many employees who direct the movement of trains, who handle the mail, the baggage and the express, who keep its voluminous records and who serve passengers and patrons in countless ways. They function under the direction of the general manager, who heads the Station Company's organization.

Directing the movement of the trains and the redcap service, is the duty of the stationmaster and his staff. His office, like those of other supervisory officers of the company, keeps in close touch with activities everywhere on the property by means of a private loudspeaker system and "TelAutographs"—automatic message-writing machines.

The chief engineer and his staff care for the buildings, the electrical systems, the air-conditioning systems as well as the 12.81 miles of tracks and governing signals. Employee payrolls, tax payments and other financial records are the responsibility of the auditor-secretary and his staff. The general baggage and mail agent also has a large organization for handling the huge volume of mail and baggage which passes through the station daily.

Close teamwork among these different departments is the key to smooth performance of Chicago Union Station's countless daily duties.

(1) LAKE STREET INTERLOCKING TOWER

(2) WORKING AN INTERLOCKER

(3) THE ELECTRICAL SUBSTATION

(4) SORTING U.S. MAIL

(5) LOADING EXPRESS

These pictures of "behind the scenes" at Chicago Union Station featured the interlocking towers and sorting of U.S. Mail and express. *Pennsylvania Railroad baggage tag, Author collection*

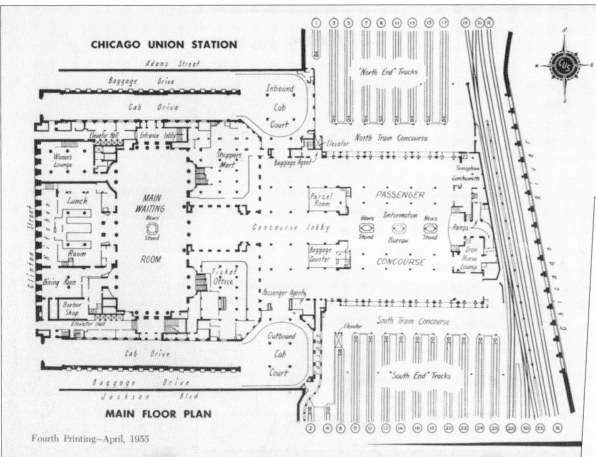

This diagram shows the main floor plan of Chicago Union Station including the North and South train concourse. *Gulf, Mobile & Ohio Railroad pocket timetable, Author collection*

The flagship of Pennsylvania Railroad's Blue Ribbon fleet was the Broadway Limited operating over the great "broad way" between New York and Chicago. In celebration of the train's 50th Anniversary, it is pictured breaking through a paper banner departing Union Station on its eastbound journey in 1952. *Courtesy Lake Forest College Special Collections*

Chicago Union Station Gate Sign 24 displayed the 5 pm departure for the Broadway Limited to New York City, circa 1958. *Courtesy Lake Forest College Special Collections*

Observation car "Mountain View" on the Broadway Limited was photographed at Englewood, Illinois, passing under a signal bridge with PRR-style position light signals, circa 1960. *Courtesy Lake Forest College Special Collections*

Inspired by industrial designer Raymond Loewy, the Baldwin Locomotive Works built DR-6-4-2000 "Sharknose" diesels for the Pennsylvania Railroad in 1947. The Blue Ribbon Fleet passenger train posed at the Chicago 12th Street coach yard in this late-1940s publicity photo with Chicago skyline in the background. *Courtesy Lake Forest College Special Collections*

Publicity photo at Union Station shows the Olympian Hiawatha departure as 3:30 pm on Track 15 to Seattle and Tacoma. The sign lists the train's major stops (left) and car numbers (right). Separate check-in desks were provided for Olympian Hiawatha sleeping car and coach passengers, circa 1950. *Courtesy Lake Forest College Special Collections*

This interior publicity photo highlights the dining car on Milwaukee Road's Twin Cities Hiawatha. Note the wait staff posed against the wall while the dining car Stewart stood in the doorway. During the early and middle 20th Century it was common practice in railroad passenger service for a white supervisor to direct all African-American crews. *Courtesy Lake Forest College Special Collections*

Another interior publicity photo featured the "Skytop" parlor-lounge car on Milwaukee Road's Hiawatha. Styled by Wisconsin industrial designer Brooks Stevens and built by the railroad's Milwaukee Shops in 1948, the streamlined car's curved ends were 90 percent glass, with comfortable chairs and sofa facing the back window so passengers could enjoy passing views. *Courtesy Lake Forest College Special Collections*

Great Northern Railway's premier passenger train was the Empire Builder, operating between Chicago, Twin Cities and Seattle-Portland. In 1947 it was photographed passing through the fog west of Chicago. Leading the train were two new E7A diesel locomotives from General Motors' Electro-Motive Division. *Courtesy Lake Forest College Special Collections*

A Northern Pacific Railway Stewardess-nurse posed near the round-end observation car of its famous North Coast Limited (Chicago-Seattle) at Union Station's south train shed. *Courtesy Lake Forest College Special Collections*

Chicago Union Station had two back-to-back stub terminals. Nine stub-end tracks formed the north concourse serving Milwaukee Road trains, and after 1955, Union Pacific's "City" fleet. The south concourse had 13 stub-end tracks and hosted trains of the Burlington Route, Pennsylvania Railroad and tenant Gulf, Mobile & Ohio Railroad. Pictured from the left are Burlington locomotive 9943B, and Burlington "Silver Garden" coach-buffet-dome-lounge car on Train 12, combined Nebraska Zephyr-Kansas City Zephyr, April 16, 1969. *J.M. Gruber collection*

A quartet of Burlington locomotives were smoking it up out of Union Station leading the westbound Morning Zephyr to the Twin Cities in May of 1966. Burlington's Railway Express Building (above first locomotive), referred to as QXT, and was located north of Roosevelt Road and east of Canal Street. *J.M. Gruber collection*

Burlington Route travel guide (August 1950) promoted the Morning and Afternoon Vista-Dome Twin Zephyrs between Chicago and the Twin Cities. *Author collection*

BURLINGTON'S TWIN *Zephyrs*
FEATURING THE *Vista-Dome*
MORNING AND AFTERNOON
between
CHICAGO · ST. PAUL · MINNEAPOLIS

The Diesel-powered, stainless steel Twin Zephyrs provide a new high in Chicago-St. Paul-Minneapolis service. These Zephyrs—the first regular trains to feature Vista-Dome cars—bring America a new conception of train travel at its thrilling best.

Each of the Twin Zephyrs consists of a luxurious parlor-observation car with Vista-Dome; a colorful diner; four spacious coaches, each with Vista-Dome; a beautifully appointed club-lounge; and a 4,000 H.P. Diesel locomotive.

Each of the spacious Vista-Domes has 24 deep-cushioned seats, enclosed in non-glare, heat-resistant safety glass. Here passengers ride in air-conditioned comfort and enjoy an unobstructed panorama of the country-side. Seats are not reserved, so all passengers may have an opportunity to enjoy this treat.

Smooth starting and stopping of the train comes from a combination of Diesel power, tight-lock couplers which eliminate slack between cars, roller bearings and electro-pneumatic disc brakes. Hydraulic shock absorbers, rubber-cushioning, and other unseen innovations, provide velvet-smooth riding qualities.

Air-conditioning is scientifically designed for greater comfort, each car having individually-controlled temperature and humidity. Telephone service between diner and club-lounge. Radio outlets in all cars, and public address system throughout the train.

Super-speed, super-comfort, super-luxury, but NO EXTRA FARE.

FOUR OTHER FINE TRAINS DAILY

EMPIRE BUILDER—Buffet-observation-lounge car, sleeping cars, dining car, lounge-coffee shop, reclining chair-coaches.

BLACK HAWK—Buffet-lounge car, sleeping cars, reclining chair-coaches.

NORTH COAST LIMITED—Buffet-observation-lounge car; standard and tourist sleeping cars, dining car, Day-Nite coaches.

ORIENTAL LIMITED—Observation-lounge car, standard and tourist sleeping cars, dining car, reclining chair-coaches.

Eight miles from Union Station is La Vergne, Illinois, the east end of Burlington's triple-track raceway through the suburbs to Aurora, Illinois. In April of 1970, the eastbound Denver Zephyr hurried past the Penn Central locomotive for its final destination at Chicago Union Station. *J. M. Gruber collection*

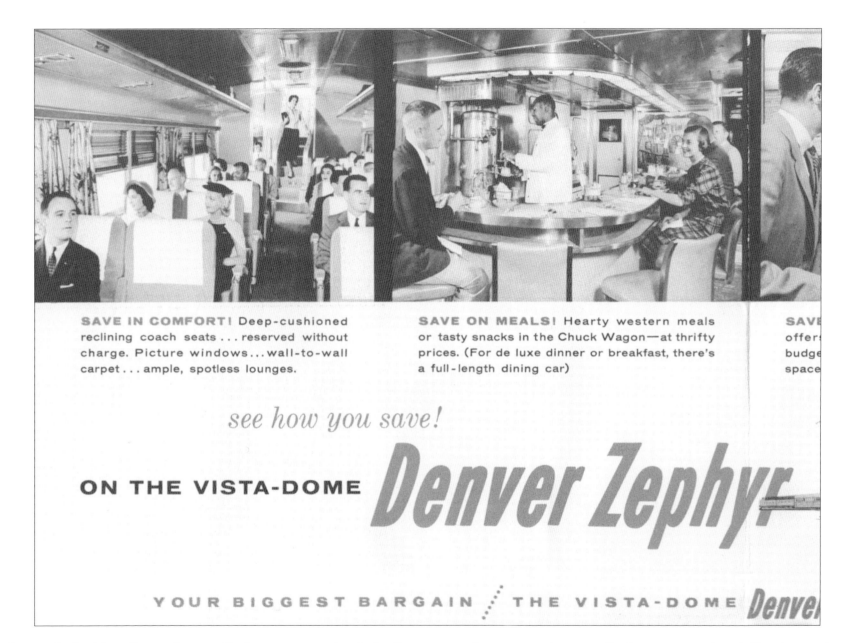

SAVE IN COMFORT! Deep-cushioned reclining coach seats ... reserved without charge. Picture windows ... wall-to-wall carpet ... ample, spotless lounges.

SAVE ON MEALS! Hearty western meals or tasty snacks in the Chuck Wagon—at thrifty prices. (For de luxe dinner or breakfast, there's a full-length dining car)

SAVE offers budge space

see how you save!

ON THE VISTA-DOME **Denver Zephyr**

YOUR BIGGEST BARGAIN / THE VISTA-DOME *Denver*

In 1956, the Vista-Dome Denver Zephyr was considered the finest overnight train in America. Burlington introduced Slumbercoaches (budget sleeping rooms) on the train, and the mid-train "Chuck Wagon" dome-dormitory-buffet lounge car featured Colorado and Western décor. *Author collection*

The Denver Zephyrs carried the blunt-end Vista-Dome parlor-buffet-observation car "Silver Chateau." *Author collection*

In July of 1968, J. M. Gruber photographed the westbound California Zephyr, led by E8 locomotive 9966, crossing over to the center track at La Grange, Illinois.

CHICAGO · SAN FRANCISCO

THE VISTA-DOME

California Zephyr

BURLINGTON · RIO GRANDE
WESTERN PACIFIC

California Zephyr travel brochure, circa 1955, offered photos of the route and train, which traversed the magnificent Colorado Rockies and awesome Feather River Canyon in daylight for passengers to enjoy. *Author collection*

Northern Pacific Railway's leading passenger train was the North Coast Limited to the Pacific Northwest. In July of 1968, J. M. Gruber photographed the westbound train at La Grange, Illinois, led by Burlington E9 locomotive 9989B. *J. M. Gruber collection*

Burlington provided motive power for both Great Northern and Northern Pacific trains between Chicago and the Twin Cities. In August of 1967, Burlington E-units were leading the westbound North Coast Limited and combined Afternoon Zephyr near Eola (Indian word meaning "North Wind") between Naperville and Aurora, Illinois. *J.M. Gruber collection; NP coach reservation, Author collection*

VISTA-DOME
NORTHERN PACIFIC

NORTH COAST LIMITED

NORTHERN PACIFIC RAILWAY

Coach Reservation

Present this form when boarding train

SEAT NO._____ CAR_____ TRAIN NO._____ DEP. TIME_____

TICKET OR CODE NO._____ GOOD ONLY ON_____

FROM_____ DATE_____

TO_____

NUMBER OF CHILDREN UNDER 5 YEARS_____ DESTINATION_____

F.CRC-1

CONDUCTOR'S PUNCH ○

If trip is cancelled notify agent at once

Aurora, Illinois, is 38 miles from Chicago Union Station and the terminus for Burlington commuter trains to the western suburbs. In June of 1966, J. M. Gruber photographed the westbound Empire Builder in its striking orange-and-green colors, led by Burlington E9 locomotive 9990. After the conductor's "Hi-Ball," the Empire Builder continued along Burlington's Mississippi River Line, "Where Nature Smiles 300 Miles," to the Twin Cities.

South of Union Station, a heavyweight Burlington coach provided an interesting contrast coupled to modern stainless steel coaches. Note Burlington's "Everywhere West" slogan, and Illinois Central's "Main Line of Mid America" on boxcars along with the ever-present water towers atop Chicago buildings in the background, circa 1950s. *J. M. Gruber collection*

Pennsylvania Railroad's Polk Street Freight House formed the backdrop in this scene. The freight house stood five stories tall and covered 7.5 acres with 18 covered sidings to load and unload freight cars. Pennsy E8 locomotive 4273 was backing its train into Union Station when J. M. Gruber took the photo in February of 1969.

Pennsylvania Railroad heavyweight cars were photographed being moved to the Pennsy coach yards south of Union Station. Note the classic automobiles, likely belonging to railroad employees, circa late 1950s. *J. M. Gruber collection*

The South Wind was a Chicago to Miami passenger train operating every third day over four participating railroads. The Pennsylvania Railroad operated the train from Chicago to Louisville, Kentucky (313 miles); The Louisville & Nashville Railroad forwarded it to Birmingham, Alabama, via Nashville (490 miles); Atlantic Coast Line Railroad ran it from Birmingham to Jacksonville, Florida (389 miles) and Florida East Coast Railway took it the last 366 miles to Miami. The South Wind departed Chicago Union Station on a cold winter day led by Atlantic Coast Line E7 motive power, circa 1950s. *J. M. Gruber collection*

This is the continuation of the same South Wind train (previous photo) with Louisville & Nashville coach 3257 carrying the marker lights, circa 1950s. *J. M. Gruber collection*

Gulf, Mobile & Ohio's E7 locomotive 103A, painted in handsome maroon-and-red livery, led a long Chicago-St. Louis train with Missouri Pacific baggage car behind the diesels. Look behind the signals (above third baggage car) to see the Empire Builder and North Coast Limited trainsets in the coach yards. *J. M. Gruber collection*

Inspired by a poem, "Song of Hiawatha" by Henry Wadsworth Longfellow, Milwaukee Road's Hiawatha became a legend, known for speed, comfort and dependability, operating between Chicago, Milwaukee and the Twin Cities. Pictured is the Hiawatha at Glenview, Illinois, circa 1960s. *J. M. Gruber photo*

Wisconsin-based industrial designer Brooks Stevens best defined the post-war era with his Skytop parlor-lounge cars for Hiawatha train service. The glass-roofed lounge area, pictured here at Glenview, Illinois, in July of 1968, offered the best views with comfortable sofas and chairs. *J. M. Gruber collection*

Chicago Union Station's north train sheds were under construction when this photo of Milwaukee Road's Skytop parlor-lounge car "Coon Rapids" was taken in June of 1966. *J. M. Gruber collection*

Pioneer Limited-Train 4 had arrived at Union Station's north train sheds from the Twin Cites on its overnight run with Railway Post Office cars. In the same picture Milwaukee Road locomotive 105C was leading an outbound suburban train, circa 1960s. *J.M. Gruber collection*

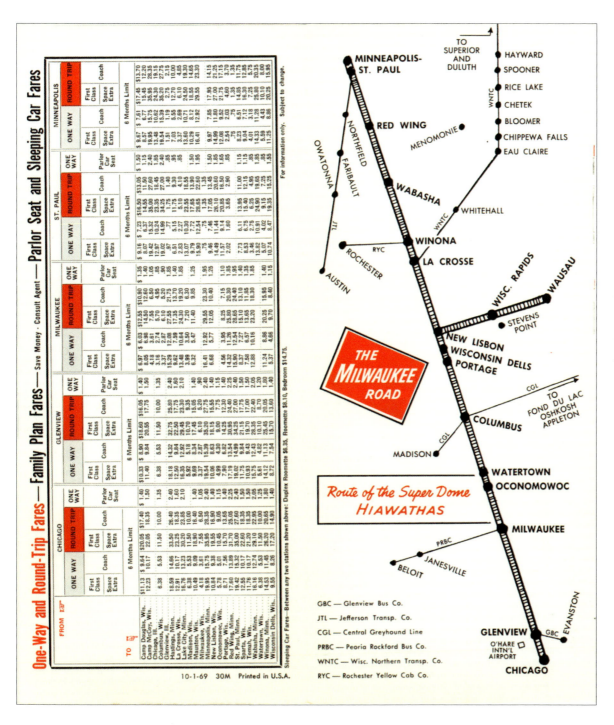

Milwaukee Road fare schedule and route map (October 1969) for the Super Dome Hiawathas and Pioneer Limited between Chicago, Milwaukee and the Twin Cities. *Author collection*

Milwaukee Road's Western Avenue Yard was located three miles from Union Station, immediately west-northwest of Tower A-2 on the north side of the mainline. Western Avenue serviced and stored both intercity and suburban equipment. In November of 1968, J. M. Gruber photographed E9 locomotive 32A at the Western Avenue diesel house. Today, Metra uses this facility to service and store part of its suburban fleet.

From 1946 to 1948, locomotive builder Fairbanks-Morse (FM) delivered 14 A-units and six B-units to the Milwaukee Road. However, due to space limitations at FM's Beloit, Wisconsin, plant the streamlined units were manufactured at General Electric's Erie, Pennsylvania, facility and became known as "Erie Built." FM locomotive 11B was assigned to Western Avenue in the early 1960s and photographed near Tower A-2. *J. M. Gruber collection*

On October 30, 1955, Union Pacific terminated its joint train operating agreement with Chicago & North Western, favoring Milwaukee Road to become its operating partner for passenger trains between Omaha and Chicago. In June of 1969, J. M. Gruber photographed a combined Union Pacific "City" train led by Milwaukee Road FP45 locomotive 5 at Western Avenue in Chicago. *J. M. Gruber collection*

By the early 1960s most American passenger railroads had declining ridership due to increased airline travel and private automobiles. The railroads' final loss of revenue came in September of 1967, when the United States Post Office transferred most mail from trains to air and truck routes. Seeking ways to improve revenue at Chicago Union Station, officials negotiated air rights for new buildings over the station's north train sheds. In April of 1969 the concourse building was demolished for a new 35-story office building. *J. M. Gruber collection; Chicago Union Station postcard, Author collection*

Chicago Stations – Gates to Everywhere

Dearborn Street Station

Dearborn Station, located at Polk and Dearborn Street, was the Chicago terminal for the Santa Fe Railway and its fleet of Chief trains. Wearing the proud Santa Fe red-and-silver Warbonnet colors, the San Francisco Chief awaited departure from Dearborn Station, circa 1960s. *J. M. Gruber collection; Dearborn Station postcard, Author collection*

One of Chicago's great train-watching locations was the Roosevelt Road viaduct overlooking Dearborn Station. Pictured is a Wabash Railway Express Agency car and Pullman sleeper "Blue Gazelle." Also in the photo is Santa Fe Alco RS1 switching a train with a Big Dome car. Notice the Lee Overalls sign above the train shed, a familiar landmark often seen in photos of Dearborn Station. *J. M. Gruber collection*

Santa Fe Fairbanks-Morse H-12-44 switched heavyweight chair cars through the canyons of freight houses near Dearborn Station, circa 1960s. *J. M. Gruber collection*

Another day in the late 1950s at Dearborn Station saw Erie business car 4 being switched, while on the next track a Santa Fe passenger train was boarding for its westbound journey. *J. M. Gruber collection*

The Chicago & Eastern Illinois freight house near Dearborn Station shows stacked crates for loading on the Frisco boxcar as Erie coaches were switched in the foreground, circa 1950s. *J. M. Gruber collection*

Santa Fe business car 31 was on the rear of a train at Dearborn Station, no date available. *J. M. Gruber collection*

J. M. Gruber photographed Santa Fe Alco PA1 in its twilight years and still dressed in the proud Warbonnet livery, fronting a passenger train out of Dearborn Station, February 4, 1968.

Chicago & Eastern Illinois Railroad's E7 locomotive 1100 in streamlined blue-and-gold colors led a train with head-end mail and express past the Chicago River's South Branch at 21st Street Junction in Chicago, circa 1956. *J. M. Gruber collection*

By the late 1960s passenger train ridership in America had fallen on hard times, with most trains carrying few passengers. Many locomotives also lost their Art Deco styling, like this Chicago & Eastern Illinois 1600-series FP7, painted somber dark blue, at Dearborn Station. *J. M. Gruber collection*

Monon's Thoroughbred (Chicago-Louisville) looked fine in the red-and-gray paint scheme at Dearborn Station, circa 1950s. The word Monon derived from the Potawatomi Indian language meaning "Swift Running." Monon billed itself as the "Hoosier Line" in reference to Indiana University athletic teams. *J. M. Gruber collection; ticket, Author collection*

Pictured is a Monon train leaving Dearborn Station, circa late 1950s. Notable is the Chicago & Eastern Illinois freight house located at the southeast corner of Clark Street and Roosevelt Road. Also visible is the Baltimore & Ohio clock tower at Grand Central Station (center top). *J. M. Gruber collection*

Grand Trunk Western operated the Maple Leaf from Chicago's Dearborn Station to Union Station in Toronto, Ontario. Shown is Grand Trunk Western dining car 1245 leaving Dearborn Station on the Maple Leaf circa 1950s. *J. M. Gruber collection*

On February 26, 1950, Wabash Railroad introduced dome cars for the streamlined Blue Bird so passengers could enjoy dome views on the Chicago-St. Louis route. The Blue Bird is shown leaving Dearborn Station with the Chicago Board of Trade Building in the background. *J. M. Gruber collection*

Baltimore & Ohio's (B&O) Capitol Limited was the biggest "name" train using Grand Central Station at Wells and Harrison Streets in the south Loop. Grand Central was also the terminus for Chicago Great Western, Pere Marquette and Soo Line passenger trains. Pictured outbound is a B&O heavyweight train led by F3 locomotive 4460 with Grand Central Station's magnificent train shed in the background, circa 1958. *J. M. Gruber collection; Grand Central Station postcard, Author collection*

In this photo, a B&O train had both heavyweight and streamlined coaches operating south of Grand Central Station. Note the late 1950s automobiles mixed with Rock Island suburban cars in the background. *J. M. Gruber collection*

Baltimore & Ohio's "Clover Hollow" was originally Pullman-built (eight-section sleeper and five double bedrooms) and streamlined in 1938 for Capitol Limited service. It received the handsome B&O royal blue, silver and gold-pin-striped colors in 1948 (a paint scheme that became one of the all-time streamliner classics) pictured on the Washington Express departing Chicago, circa 1954. *J. M. Gruber collection*

In the decade before Amtrak, Chesapeake & Ohio (C&O) passenger trains used Grand Central Station for their Chicago-Grand Rapids, Michigan service. Pictured is C&O dining car "Hanover Tavern," originally built by the Pullman Company in 1929 as car No. 971, "Rising Sun Tavern." At that time, C&O named its cars for people, events and places in the life of George Washington. Photographed circa 1960s at Chicago. *J. M. Gruber collection*

The Soo Line offered passenger service on the Laker between Chicago-Superior-Duluth, operating as Trains 17 and 18, later changed to Trains 3 and 4 in 1959. Soo Line never streamlined their coaches like other railroads did, and operated with heavyweight equipment shown in this late 1950s photo. Soo passenger trains terminated at Grand Central Station before moving to Illinois Central's Central Station in 1963. The Laker made its final run on January 16, 1965. *J. M. Gruber collection*

180—Air View Showing Illinois Central Depot in Foreground, Chicago

Illinois Central Railroad's premier passenger train was the all-Pullman Panama Limited operating from Chicago to New Orleans on a fast overnight schedule. Beginning in 1942, Illinois Central passenger trains wore the striking brown-and-orange-with-yellow-stripe scheme developed by Electro-Motive Division's Styling Section and shown here at Indian Oakes, Illinois, in October of 1964. *J. M. Gruber collection; IC Central Station postcard, Author collection*

This view shows the Panama Limited led by E7 locomotive 4012 under a signal bridge along the Illinois Central mainline near Chicago, in June of 1968. *J. M. Gruber collection*

Kensington Station, a commuter rail station on the south side of Chicago (115th Street and Cottage Grove Avenue) in the Pullman neighborhood, served Illinois Central electrics and South Shore commuter trains. On March 5, 1951, an Illinois Central passenger train with head-end mail and express cars was near Kensington. *J. M. Gruber collection*

Illinois Central (IC) and New York Central jointly operated the Indianapolis Special between Chicago and Indianapolis, Indiana. The train departed from IC Central Station with IC crews to Kankakee, Illinois. New York Central crews then took the train to Indianapolis. Pictured is the Indianapolis Special at Kankakee, Illinois, circa 1964. *J. M. Gruber collection*

In this view from the Roosevelt Road overpass, New York Central E8 locomotive 4039 led a train with mostly mail and express cars. Chicago's urban skyline highlights La Salle Street Station and Board of Trade building towering in the background. *J. M. Gruber collection; La Salle Street Station postcard, Author collection*

110—La Salle Street Station, Chicago

New York Central's mail and express facility south of La Salle Station was a busy yard with different types of equipment, including Railway Express Agency refrigerator car, storage mail cars, baggage-express cars and milk car, circa 1950s. *J. M. Gruber collection*

Here are your tickets for
the New York Central

M...

The Central
is happy to welcome you
aboard and wishes you
a pleasant journey

Between New York and Chicago
go **20th Century Limited**
LUXURY SERVICE AT NO EXTRA COST!
The famed "Century" is still the most comfortable
way to go. Enjoy relaxing lounge cars, superb dining
car service, your own Sleeping Car or Sleepercoach
private room accommodations.

New York Central E8 locomotive 4049 looked impressive wearing the "Lighting Stripe" paint scheme and leading the 20th Century Limited at Englewood Union Station (63rd Street), circa 1960s. *J. M. Gruber collection; ticket folder, Author collection*

New York Central E8 locomotive 4044 also wore the "Lighting Stripe" colors fronting a passenger train in suburban Chicago, circa 1960s. *J. M. Gruber collection; NYC decal, Author collection*

The Rock Island Railroad and Southern Pacific Lines operated the Golden State passenger train between Chicago and Los Angeles. On a cold, clear Chicago winter day the Golden State had departed LaSalle Station, led by Rock Island E8 in maroon-and-yellow wings scheme, circa 1960s. *J. M. Gruber collection; ticket folder, Author collection*

Another Rock Island passenger train was leaving La Salle Station with E8 locomotive 645 in maroon colors with white lettering, passing New York Central's mail and express yard, circa 1960s. *J. M. Gruber collection*

Rock Island's Peorian-Train 11 (former Peoria Rocket) was outbound from Chicago to Peoria, Illinois, circa 1970s. *J. M. Gruber collection; ticket, Author collection*

In this 1960s photo, Nickel Plate Road's eastbound New Yorker eased away from La Salle Station with modernized, heavyweight diner-lounge car 126. *J. M. Gruber collection; ticket folder, Author collection*

A vintage 1956 Chevrolet posed in front of Nickel Plate Road baggage-express car south of La Salle Station. Notice the green Railway Express Agency trailers behind the baggage car and "Ship Santa Fe – Serving the West" sign behind the building, circa 1960s. *J. M. Gruber collection*

The Twin Cities 400 with parlor-solarium car 7201 was outbound from North Western Station in June of 1963. C&NW parlor-solarium cars 7200 and 7201 had rounded ends instead of the traditional, teardrop style on most parlor cars. Both cars were used exclusively on the Twin Cities 400. *J. M. Gruber collection; 400 drink coaster, Author collection*

The North Western Limited operated overnight between Chicago and the Twin Cities via Milwaukee. The Chicago & North Western public timetable, July 27, 1952, listed the trains as 405 and 406, departing Chicago and the Twin Cities respectively at 11 pm. Pictured is the North Western Limited led by E8A locomotive 5024 arriving at North Western Station in Chicago, circa 1950s. *J. M. Gruber collection*

Streamliners to Amtrak – The Rainbow Era

On May 1, 1971, the newly created, government-sponsored Amtrak assumed operation of most U.S. passenger trains. Shown is the Nationwide Schedules of Intercity Passenger Service, Amtrak's first public timetable, effective May 1, 1971. *Author collection*

The Rainbow Era.

In 1968, a young attorney named Anthony Haswell founded the National Association of Railroad Passengers (NARP), a Washington lobby group whose purpose was to save the passenger trains. NARP began lobbying Congress, the Department of Transportation, and the Federal Railroad Administration on behalf of passenger trains. After much effort the NARP lobbying worked, and from that success came the Railroad Passenger Service Act (Railpax), which Congress passed October 14, 1970. On October 30, 1970, President Nixon signed Public Law 91-518, and the National Railroad Passenger Corporation (NRPC) was created. All railroads that operated passenger trains when the new law was signed had until May 1, 1971, to become members of the NRPC, or continue to run their own passenger trains. The NRPC membership price was either cash, or passenger equipment/services based on half the road's passenger losses for the last full year of operation (1970), or purchase of common stock in the new company. The biggest advantage to joining NRPC was, of course, relief from the financial burden of maintaining passenger service. Most railroads joined, although four opted out and continued to operate passenger trains on their own: Southern, Rio Grande, Rock Island, and Georgia Railroad.

The advertising firm of Lippencott & Marguiles created the name for the new passenger carrier, AMTRAK (American Travel by Track), and developed the corporate colors of red, white and blue and the well-known Amtrak inverted arrow logo. Amtrak's arrow logo was replaced in the year 2000 with its wave-like "travel mark," introduced concurrent with the launch of its satisfaction guarantee program and in anticipation of the high-speed *Acela Express*.

Amtrak's early years are often called the "Rainbow Era," referring to hand-me-down engines, coaches and sleepers from the various railroads that formed the colorful consists of early Amtrak trains.

By mid-1971, the passenger carrier began purchasing some of the equipment it had leased, including 286 second-hand E and F units, 30 GG1 electric locomotives, and 1,290 passenger cars, and continued leasing even more motive power. The "Rainbow Era" was short-lived, and by 1974 the new red, blue and silver color scheme was on most Amtrak equipment. Newly purchased locomotives and rolling stock began appearing, too—SDP40Fs from EMD in 1972, French-built Turboliner trainsets in 1973, and new Amfleet coaches from the Budd Company in 1975. In 1972, Amtrak began using Chicago Union Station's former head house as their Midwest Chicago hub. After years of service the station was showing its age, and in 1991 Amtrak began a $32 million, two-year passenger improvement project that included renewal of the station's public areas and baggage handling system. The Beaux-Arts style architecture remains but with a modern-day look including enlarged concourse waiting areas, improved lighting, better train-gate access and Metropolitan Lounge for sleeping car passengers. The Chicago Union Station Company, a subsidiary of Amtrak, owns the station. According to the *Chicago Tribune* (October 4, 2010), "Chicago Union Station averages 55 Amtrak long-distance and regional trains daily." In addition, six of Metra's 11 commuter routes hub from the station, for a combined total of 140,000 passengers daily." Today, with higher automobile gas prices, increased traffic congestion on city expressways and interstate highways, combined with extra fees imposed by airlines, Americans are realizing that our country needs more than ever to invest in commuter rail and long-distance passenger trains. As our country's leaders give the signal to "Go Green," the future looks bright for Amtrak and Chicago Union Station in the 21st Century.

Among the most colorful trains in Amtrak's "Rainbow Era" (circa 1971) were those of newly merged Burlington Northern. Pictured is locomotive 9943 in Cascade-green-and-white, fronting the Empire Builder with former Great Northern "Big Sky Blue" cars in suburban Chicago. *J. M. Gruber photo; BN timetable, Author collection*

In its first year of operation (1971), Amtrak kept the Denver Zephyr as a separate train between Chicago and Denver with its own column in Amtrak timetables, but the train was eventually combined with the San Francisco Zephyr. Pictured is the Denver Zephyr in a Christmas card scene at La Grange, Illinois. *John Mummert photo*

Shown is the continuation of the Denver Zephyr (previous photo) as passengers enjoyed penthouse views in the Vista-Dome observation car passing through La Grange, Illinois, circa 1971. *John Mummert photo*

During the early Amtrak era the San Francisco Zephyr (SFZ) made its debut on June 11, 1972, operating between Chicago, Denver, Salt Lake City and Oakland, California, with bus connections to San Francisco. Amtrak's timetable (September 10, 1972) listed the SFZ as Trains 5 and 6, operating Sunday, Wednesday and Friday from Chicago. John Mummert photographed the San Francisco Zephyr with Burlington locomotive 9966 leading at Downers Grove, Illinois, circa 1972.

Amtrak's San Francisco Zephyr with two Union Pacific cars in tow made a station stop at Aurora, Illinois, before its final terminus at Chicago Union Station, circa 1972. *John Mummert photo*

Pictured is Amtrak "Silver Chalet" dormitory-buffet-lounge car (formerly owned by Western Pacific Railroad) in Amtrak's new red-blue-and-silver scheme and a Burlington Northern coach in Cascade-green-and-white at Aurora, Illinois, circa 1972. This photo is a good example of "rainbow trains" with some equipment painted in the colors of their former owner railroads. *John Mummert photo*

Another close-up view shows Amtrak's "Silver Chalet" dormitory-buffet-lounge car on the San Francisco Zephyr at Aurora, Illinois, circa 1972. *John Mummert photo*

On an overcast Chicago day, John Mummert photographed the San Francisco Zephyr led by Burlington locomotive 9969 under the signal bridge in Downer's Grove, Illinois, circa 1972. *Amtrak travel guide, Author collection*

This view features a former Milwaukee Road Super Dome car used by Amtrak on San Francisco Zephyr trainsets east of Ogden, Utah. West of Ogden, the SFZ used Southern Pacific (SP) home-built dome cars, the only domes SP would allow on its routes until the late 1970s. *John Mummert photo*

Chesapeake & Ohio's E8 locomotive 1471 led an unidentified passenger train out of Chicago. According to Amtrak Consolidated Regional Timetable, September 10, 1972, this train was likely the George Washington, departing Chicago at 2 pm daily for Washington, D.C. *J. M. Gruber collection; Amtrak timetable, Author collection*

Between 1973 and 1975, Amtrak purchased six French "Turboliner" trains with aircraft-type turbine engines. The five-car trainsets carried 296 passengers and included two power cars, two coaches and a bar-grill car. They operated from Chicago to St. Louis, and eventually to Port Huron and Detroit, Michigan, Toledo, Ohio and Milwaukee, Wisconsin. Pictured is a Chicago-Milwaukee corridor train led by Amtrak locomotive 405, passing one of the new turbo trains conducting test runs along that route. *J. M. Gruber photo; postcard, Author collection*

Amtrak's first order for new SDP40F diesels from Electro-Motive Division was in 1973-1974. The SDP40Fs were six-axle units with covered cowl design adapted from the FP45s used by Santa Fe Railway and Milwaukee Road. The SDP40Fs proved unsuccessful for Amtrak due to alleged tracking problems and were replaced with the more popular F40PH locomotives. Shown is Amtrak's Southwest Limited departing Chicago Union Station circa 1974, led by SDP40F locomotive 542. *J. M. Gruber collection*

Chicago Commuter Trains – Riding the 5:16 Express

After the 1970 "Hill Lines" merger, Burlington Northern (BN) continued to operate suburban service from Chicago Union Station through the western suburbs, 38 miles to Aurora. In this 1973 scene, BN E9A locomotive 9983 departed Union Station with its westbound commuter train, the Sears Tower standing tall in the background. *J. M. Gruber photo*

Burlington Northern had two paint schemes for freight and passenger locomotives. The passenger scheme was a green carbody with white nose stripes, and on the sides a wide angle stripe that looked like a "hockey stick," as pictured on E9 locomotive 9904. For decades the block-long Pennsylvania Railroad Polk Street freight house served as a backdrop for photographing trains from the Roosevelt Road overpass. The freight house was being demolished in 1974 when J. M. Gruber took this photo.

Western Avenue was the second westbound Burlington commuter stop from Union Station. In the early 1970s, Burlington E8 locomotive 9941B, leading stainless steel bi-level cars, heeled into the curve at Western Avenue. *J. M. Gruber photo*

Burlington had power cars in commuter consists when pulled by E-units that were steam generator equipped. The power cars were converted coaches with a Cummins diesel engine and a 65 KW generator to supply head-end power to the bi-level commuter trains. Power car modifications included a rounded roof, tight-lock couplers, roller-bearing trucks and silver paint as shown behind E8 locomotive 9945A. All power cars were retired in 1974. *J. M. Gruber collection*

A Burlington commuter train with bi-level cars led by E8 locomotive 9948B passed under the block signal bridge in Chicago's western suburbs. *J. M. Gruber collection; Burlington Route suburban timetable, Paul Clusen collection*

Burlington Route

EFFECTIVE
APRIL 24, 1960
Chicago Daylight Saving Time

EASTBOUND

Suburban Service

Union Passenger Station
CANAL AT JACKSON BLVD.
Phone FRanklin 2-6700

City Ticket Office
Bankers Building
ADAMS AT CLARK ST.
Phone WAbash 2-2345

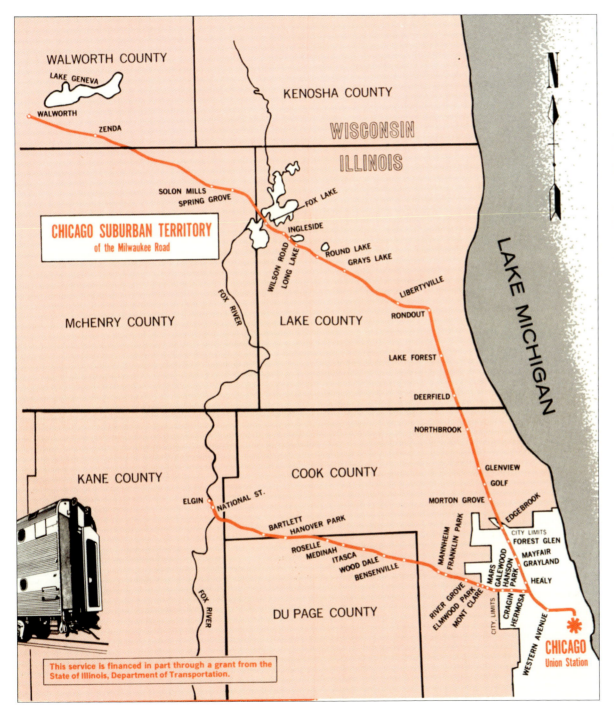

WALWORTH COUNTY
LAKE GENEVA
WALWORTH
ZENDA

KENOSHA COUNTY

WISCONSIN
ILLINOIS

SOLON MILLS
SPRING GROVE
FOX LAKE
INGLESIDE

CHICAGO SUBURBAN TERRITORY
of the Milwaukee Road

WILSON ROAD
LONG LAKE
ROUND LAKE
GRAYS LAKE

FOX RIVER

McHENRY COUNTY
LAKE COUNTY
LIBERTYVILLE
RONDOUT
LAKE FOREST
DEERFIELD

NORTHBROOK

KANE COUNTY
COOK COUNTY
GLENVIEW
GOLF

ELGIN
NATIONAL ST.
MORTON GROVE
EDGEBROOK

BARTLETT
HANOVER PARK
CITY LIMITS
FOREST GLEN

ROSELLE
MEDINAH
ITASCA
WOOD DALE
BENSENVILLE
MANNHEIM
FRANKLIN PARK
MAYFAIR
GRAYLAND

MARS
GALEWOOD
HANSON PARK
HEALY

FOX RIVER
RIVER GROVE
ELMWOOD PARK
MONT CLARE
CITY LIMITS
CRAGIN
HERMOSA

DU PAGE COUNTY

WESTERN AVENUE

LAKE MICHIGAN

N

CHICAGO
Union Station

This service is financed in part through a grant from the
State of Illinois, Department of Transportation.

The Milwaukee Road operated two commuter lines from Chicago Union Station, as shown on this Milwaukee Road suburban territory map, circa 1973. The North Line followed the mainline to Rondout then branched Northwest to Fox Lake, Illinois, and Walworth, Wisconsin. Milwaukee's West Line served Bensenville and Elgin, Illinois. *Author collection*

Milwaukee Road F9 locomotive 93A pulled stainless steel bi-level cars on the North Line at Techny (Tower A-20) near Northbrook, Illinois, in June of 1966. *J. M. Gruber photo*

In August of 1968, this Milwaukee Road commuter train was on the West Line at Tower B-17 near Bensenville, Illinois, led by E9 locomotive 38C with one bi-level car. *J. M. Gruber photo*

The Gulf, Mobile & Ohio Railroad operated a Monday-Friday commuter train each way between Joliet and Chicago. Nicknamed "The Plug," it stopped at Lockport, Lemont, Willow Springs and Summit. Pictured is the outbound "Plug" from Union Station led by F3 locomotive 883A. *J. M. Gruber collection*

On February 1, 1968, the Pennsylvania Railroad was merged into newly formed Penn Central. The Penn Central continued to operate the Chicago-Valparaiso, Indiana, commuter trains referred to as the "Valpo Local." By that time the route was a rush-hour commuter service with two trains traveling from Valparaiso to Chicago at 5:55 am and 6:35 am, and two trains returning from Chicago to Valparaiso at 5:00 pm and 5:40 pm. In 1974, Penn Central GP7 locomotive 5956 led the train with four Pennsylvania Railroad heavyweight coaches painted Tuscan red. *J. M. Gruber collection*

One of the more interesting Rock Island paint schemes was the maroon-and-yellow "wings" livery shown here on E8 locomotive 648, leading a train of older coaches outbound from La Salle Station. *J. M. Gruber collection*

In 1964, Rock Island purchased its first Budd Company bi-level suburban cars, pictured here with E6 locomotive 630 on a suburban train. *J. M. Gruber collection*

Just out of La Salle Station, former Rocky Mountain Rocket motive power AB6 locomotive 750 led a suburban train. *J. M. Gruber collection*

Illinois Central (IC) electric commuter trains operated from downtown IC station (lower level of Prudential Building), southward from the Loop to Richton. Commuter service also included the South Chicago Branch (71st Street to 91st Street), and Kensington (115th Street to Blue Island). For many years the electric fleet consisted of steel cars built in 1926 and operated in pairs (power car with pantograph and trailer car) as shown, circa 1960s. *J. M. Gruber collection*

In 1971, Illinois Central Railroad premièred their new electric "Highliner" cars. The modern double-deckers were part of a larger 130-car order for suburban service. Pictured is car 1509 operating under electrified wires near Chicago, circa 1971. *J. M. Gruber collection*

Riding the 5:16 Express.

In the 1950s and 1960s, Chicago was home to five major commuter railroads (Burlington, Chicago & North Western, Milwaukee Road, Rock Island, and Illinois Central), plus three interurban lines (Chicago, North Shore & Milwaukee; Chicago, South Shore & South Bend; and Chicago, Aurora & Elgin). Several other railroads provided commuter service including Chicago & Western Indiana, Pennsylvania Railroad (later Penn Central), Gulf, Mobile & Ohio, and Norfolk and Western. Chicago commuter trains were known as "Scoots" on the C&NW and Milwaukee Road, "Dinkies" on the Burlington, and "Dummies" on the Rock Island.

In 1950, Burlington was the first Chicago area railroad to introduce stainless steel, bi-level suburban cars. Burlington E7 and E8 locomotives cloaked in silver paint and stainless steel led trains from Chicago Union Station west to Aurora over CB&Q's triple-track raceway. By 1961, Milwaukee Road had upgraded their Chicago commuter fleet with 40 stainless steel, bi-level cars from the Budd Company (eight cab-control cars and 32 coaches). Milwaukee Road operated two commuter routes from Union Station. The North Line followed the mainline to Rondout then branched Northwest to Fox Lake, Illinois, and Walworth, Wisconsin. Milwaukee's West Line served Bensenville and Elgin, Illinois.

In October 1956, Chicago & North Western (C&NW) President Ben Heinemann upgraded his railroad's commuter fleet, replacing steam with diesel motive power and bi-level cars to make C&NW the leading Chicago commuter carrier. In 1959, C&NW initiated push-pull commuter service in which the engine pulled the train outbound or pushed the train inbound. Eventually, other Chicago commuter lines switched to push-pull operations. This allowed for a cleaner commuter environment by keeping noisy locomotives and diesel fumes away from enclosed boarding areas at downtown stations. C&NW had three commuter lines operating from the downtown Chicago & North Western Station: west to Geneva, Illinois, north to Kenosha, Wisconsin, and northwest to Harvard, Illinois (on the 5:16 Express which I regularly took).

Rock Island provided suburban service from Chicago's La Salle Street Station to Joliet, Illinois. In 1965, the railroad received their first push-pull cars (20 bi-levels) from the Budd Company to supplement older coaches, many from the 1920s. In 1970, Rock Island received ten bi-levels from Pullman Standard painted bright red with gray roofs and a yellow stripe.

Beginning in 1856, Illinois Central (IC) had begun commuter service to Chicago's south side and south suburbs. IC electrified their suburban route in 1926. The joint terminal for Illinois Central electrics and South Shore electric trains was at Michigan and Randolph Streets in the lower level of the Prudential Building. In 1971, Illinois Central took delivery of 130 modern double-decker cars (Highliners) for suburban service.

Today, the lines of these former carriers form the core of Metra's 487.7-mile system serving more than 100 communities with 240 stations on 11 routes from five downtown Chicago stations. According to Metra's website the carrier provided dependable commuter service to 81.4 million riders in 2010 with 702 weekday trains, 296 Saturday trains and 163 Sunday trains.

Metra System map and timetable (April 1995) for Northwest Line (Chicago to Harvard) shows the 11 Metra routes from downtown Chicago. *Author collection*

Metra Territory . . .

There are a lot of interesting, educational and just plain **fun** things to do in Northeast Illinois and Metra can get you where you want to go. The 495-mile Metra system serves approximately 235 stations in the counties of Cook, DuPage, Lake, Will, McHenry and Kane.

On Metra you can reach Chicago's beautiful lakefront, museums, zoos, sporting events, shops and restaurants, concerts, special events, schools and colleges as well as quaint, historic suburbs and small towns.

In some cases, Metra can take you practically to the front door – in other cases, your destination is easily in reach via Pace buses, and/or CTA buses and trains.

Remember, on weekends and holidays, all youngsters 12-17 ride for half fare. Plus, family fares allows kids under 12 to ride free when accompanied by a fare paying adult.

A small group of adults can save 15% using a 10-ride ticket when traveling together. Or, get a group of 25 or more together and save even more on a special outing. Call us for details.

Metra
The way to really fly.

547 W. JACKSON BOULEVARD
CHICAGO, ILLINOIS 60661

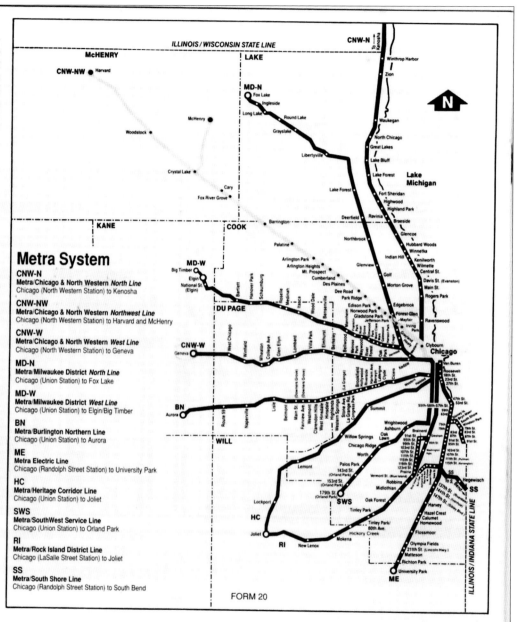

Metra System

CNW-N
Metra/Chicago & North Western *North Line*
Chicago (North Western Station) to Kenosha

CNW-NW
Metra/Chicago & North Western *Northwest Line*
Chicago (North Western Station) to Harvard and McHenry

CNW-W
Metra/Chicago & North Western *West Line*
Chicago (North Western Station) to Geneva

MD-N
Metra/Milwaukee District *North Line*
Chicago (Union Station) to Fox Lake

MD-W
Metra/Milwaukee District *West Line*
Chicago (Union Station) to Elgin/Big Timber

BN
Metra/Burlington Northern Line
Chicago (Union Station) to Aurora

ME
Metra Electric Line
Chicago (Randolph Street Station) to University Park

HC
Metra/Heritage Corridor Line
Chicago (Union Station) to Joliet

SWS
Metra/SouthWest Service Line
Chicago (Union Station) to Orland Park

RI
Metra/Rock Island District Line
Chicago (LaSalle Street Station) to Joliet

SS
Metra/South Shore Line
Chicago (Randolph Street Station) to South Bend

FORM 20

A Chicago & North Western (C&NW) afternoon commuter train was led by E8 locomotive 509 pulling bi-level cars. The 100-story John Hancock building is in the background, circa late 1960s. *J. M. Gruber collection*

Highland Park, Illinois, is a Chicago suburb along scenic Lake Michigan, 23 miles north of downtown North Western Station. In 1856 suburban service was established along this route and continued until 1976 when the Regional Transportation Authority (RTA) began train service. Pictured is C&NW E8A locomotive 5027-B and commuter train at Highland Park, July 26, 1968. *Courtesy Chicago & North Western Historical Society*

In 1959, C&NW initiated push-pull commuter service in which the engine pulled the train outbound or pushed the train inbound. This allowed faster commuter schedules as equipment no longer needed to be turned. And the addition of newer bi-level cars allowed the older bi-levels to be retrofitted for push-pull service. This photo shows cab control car 171 leading a commuter train at Highland Park, Illinois, circa 1960s. *Courtesy Chicago & North Western Historical Society*

Winter in Chicago can be brutal, with heavy snow, strong winds blowing off Lake Michigan and below zero freezing temperatures. On January 14, 1968, northbound Train 153, a bi-level Streamliner (Chicago-Milwaukee-Green Bay), charged ahead through the snow at Highland Park, Illinois. The first car is likely mail/baggage/tavern/lounge car 7601 or 7602. *Courtesy Chicago & North Western Historical Society*

On December 23, 1969, two C&NW trains met on the North Line. On the left an ice-covered locomotive is leading a Chicago-Kenosha train of bi-level cars past inbound Train 152 (Milwaukee-Chicago) Streamliner with coaches. *Courtesy Chicago & North Western Historical Society*

Two C&NW trains were side-by-side on a snowy New Years Eve, December 31, 1969, at Highland Park, Illinois. *Courtesy Chicago & North Western Historical Society*

C&NW F7A locomotive 4087-C is featured in this close-up photo leading Train 121 (Chicago-Milwaukee) bi-level Streamliner at Highland Park, Illinois, on June 8, 1969. *Courtesy Chicago & North Western Historical Society*

The sun was shining on C&NW motive power at West Chicago coach yards in this photo by J. M. Gruber, circa 1960s.

The Chicago & North Western Passenger Terminal at Madison & Canal Streets in downtown Chicago was built in 1911. The Terminal's 16-platform tracks handled arrivals and departures of the 400 fleet and Union Pacific City trains (until 1955). In 1987 the head house was razed and replaced by a glass office tower. In 1997 it was renamed the Ogilvie Transportation Center and currently used by Metra commuter trains. *Author collection*

In 1956, the C&NW commuter fleet, including this train arriving at North Western Station, was upgraded to modern bi-level cars built by Pullman-Standard. *Doug Wornom collection*

C&NW dispatchers and train crews referred to their commuter trains as "Scoots." Shown is F7 locomotive 4081-C leading an outbound "Scoot" during the busy Chicago rush hour. *Author collection*

C&NW liked to position their commuter trains at Clinton Interlocking for publicity photos. The bi-level fleet looked ready for the afternoon commute in this 1962 photo. *Author collection*

Another view of Clinton Interlocking featured a close-up of this C&NW bi-level train, circa 1959. *Courtesy Chicago & North Western Historical Society*

From the looks of heavy auto traffic in this 1962 publicity photo, riding the C&NW train over the Northwest Expressway (later renamed Kennedy Expressway) in Chicago was the way to commute. *Author collection*

North Western's Fleet of Commuter Streamliners Provides Unexcelled Service for 70,000 Chicago Commuters Daily.

This Chicago & North Western dining car menu, circa 1965, featured bi-level commuter train with parallel expressway auto traffic and the Chicago skyline in the background. *Author collection*

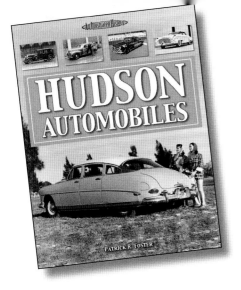

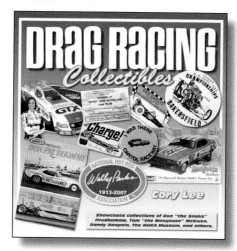

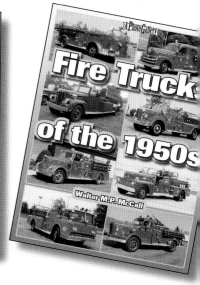

More Great Titles from Iconografix

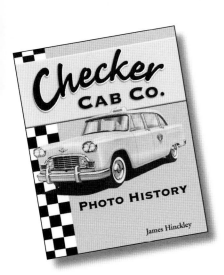

385.22
Kelly   Kelly, John.

             Chicago postwar
             passenger and
             commuter trains